Succeeding WHILE BLACK

A Blueprint For Success

MATTHEW R. DRAYTON

The opinions expressed in this manuscript are solely the opinions of the author and do not represent the opinions or thoughts of the publisher. The author has represented and warranted full ownership and/or legal right to publish all the materials in this book.

Succeeding While Black
A Blueprint for Success
All Rights Reserved.
Copyright © 2013 Matthew R. Drayton
v2.0

Cover Photo © 2013 John Covington. All rights reserved - used with permission.

This book may not be reproduced, transmitted, or stored in whole or in part by any means, including graphic, electronic, or mechanical without the express written consent of the publisher except in the case of brief quotations embodied in critical articles and reviews.

Drayton Communications

ISBN: 978-0-578-11925-0

Library of Congress Control Number: 2013931165

PRINTED IN THE UNITED STATES OF AMERICA

Acknowledgments

First I would like to thank God for watching over and blessing me for all these years. I would also like to thank my late parents Matthew (Buddy) Drayton and Juanita Simmons Drayton. Mom, you left too soon, but the years I spent with you made a major impact on my life. Dad, despite your personal struggles you were always there for me when Mom died, and you taught me a lot about how to be a man. I love and honor you both daily.

To my beautiful wife Lila--I would like to thank you for your support over the last thirty years. We have made a great team, raised a wonderful family, and achieved more than we ever thought we could. I love you. To my daughters Tiffanie and Brittny, thanks for being there for me and for providing realness to my life that has kept me grounded and focused.

To Carl Davis, my best friend from the old neighborhood, thanks for being a friend all these years. To CSM Danny Young, thanks for your friendship over the years; we have been through a lot together. You have been like a brother to me. Thanks for being a sounding board. I would also like to thank the Drayton family, the Davis family, the Chisholm family, the Brown family, the Whiting family, the Johnson family, the Evans family, the Strouse family, and the Dickens family for all their support, counsel, and love over the years.

Lastly I would like to thank all of the men and women I served with while I was in the US Army. There were so many men and women who made an impact on my life; way too many to name. You all played a major role in my life, and helped me become the man I am today. I truly appreciate your guidance, patience, and your friendship over the years.

Foreword

There is a lot of negativity associated with the term "while black." The most often heard is "driving while black." For that reason I decided to name my book *Succeeding While Black* to give a positive connotation to the "while black" phrase. *Succeeding While Black* is the first in a series of "while black" books.

Young African-Americans have a lot to be excited about. With the election of the nation's first African-American president, the sky should be the limit. While not every black child can grow up to be president, they can, and should grow up to be successful and productive members of society.

Succeeding While Black is my story of how I overcame many obstacles and a lot of adversity to have a distinguished military career, civilian career, broadcasting career, and a long successful marriage. *Succeeding While Black* is a blueprint for success by an author who became successful the hard way--through hard work, discipline, and perseverance.

The principles in this book will help many young African-Americans toward achieving their goals and becoming successful. Encourage your child to read this book today, or pick it up for someone you know.

Table of Contents

Acknowledgments	iii
Foreword	v
Introduction	ix
Gone Too Soon	1
School Days	4
Meyers Junior High	8
The Turn-Around	10
Richard Arnold High School	12
High School Senior Year	15
You're in the Army Now	19
Basic Training	23
Private Drayton Reporting for Duty	27
Germany	30
Private Johnson	36
Essentials for Success	42
Education, Education, Education	43
Punctuality	45
Attitude	47
Principles of Success	49
Discipline	50
Commitment	53
Character	56
Integrity	58

Work Ethic	60
Appearance	62
Finances	65
Social Media	68
Mentoring	70
Leadership	72
Teen Pregnancy	75
Success and the African-American	77
Conduct in the Workplace	80
The Obama Factor	83
No More Excuses	87
Summary	89

Introduction

As a black male from a poor neighborhood in Savannah, Georgia, I have seen and experienced some of the worst that society and the streets have to offer. When I joined the military in 1978, I joined to seek a better life. I couldn't afford to go to college, and I knew there had to be more to life than what I was doing.

I knew the Army would be tough, but I had to do something. Little did I know my career would span twenty-six years, and that I would retire at the highest enlisted rank of Sergeant Major. The military taught me discipline and work ethic, and provided me a formal education and the opportunity to travel all over the world. I spent sixteen years in the Army's elite Delta Force, I have been a radio station manager and on-air personality, an analyst for the Northrop Grumman Corporation, a substitute teacher, a senior Department of Defense civilian, and a small business owner.

I could have been a statistic, but I was blessed to have a family, friends, and mentors who helped me through my life's journey. With the election of an African-American president, many would ask: "Why write a book about black success?" Despite President Obama's success there are many African-American children--especially males--who are struggling to achieve success, and have lost their way.

Many African-American men will find themselves in front of a judge, in gangs, and on the streets without opportunities. Black children still trail others in almost every academic category in America.

Succeeding While Black is a blueprint for success for young (and all) African-Americans.

I wrote this book because I care about what is happening to African-Americans in this country. Our children have quit focusing on education and hard work. Many African-American adults have stopped caring about their communities, and do not help or support each other in business and the workplace.

As an African-American you will live by a different set of rules, you will be judged by a different set of standards, and you will have to fight and work harder than others for everything you get. That's just the way it is.

Those who understand this will flourish. Those who don't will struggle throughout their entire lives.

Gone Too Soon

My First Boyhood Home

June 6, 1968: As the rain poured and I watched my mother's white casket being lowered into the wet soggy ground, I had no idea what my future would hold. I was seven years old. I felt angry, alone, and afraid. Although I had spent only a few years with her, I really loved my mother. She was a heavy-set beautiful black woman with beautiful eyes, smooth chocolate skin, and thick black hair. In those few short years I spent with my mother, Juanita Drayton made a major impact on my life.

My mother taught me to read before I went to kindergarten. I was so proud and excited about reading that I would read everything in sight: signs, books--you name it, I read it. My father would get irritated at me for reading so much and tell me to be quiet. Later I would understand that learning to read at an early age would be a major benefit that would set me apart from others later in life. From now on my father, a handsome muscular light-skinned black man from a family of fourteen, would raise me by himself as an only child.

SUCCEEDING WHILE BLACK

My father was an ex-boxer who did many odd jobs before he got hired as a janitor at the Southern States Fertilizer plant in Savannah, Georgia. I did not know my father very well; I was always with my mother. I do remember my parents yelling and fighting, and I did see my father hit my mother once. My father also drank heavily on occasion. If I had to sum up my parents' marriage, I would say it was an unhappy one. I never saw my mother smile, and in those days people didn't get divorced. As we drove home from the cemetery in the rain, everything was a blur. It seemed we had driven fifty miles to and from the cemetery. I had many questions: What am I in for? Will my father drink more heavily now? Will we get along?

My mother's death caught my father by surprise and took a heavy toll on both of us, but it really hit my father hard. I think some of it was guilt, but I think mostly it was sadness because I think he truly loved her. My father was very understanding as we talked about our future together, because now it was just us two and we really needed each other. One of the first things I told my father was never to marry again. Why I said this, I don't know; maybe because I didn't want anyone to replace my mother…or maybe I was afraid that if another woman came into our lives I would be neglected. I don't know if my father took my words seriously, but he never married again. I regret ever saying those words, because every man deserves to have a loving wife to share his life with. My father and I were about to begin a ten-year journey that would shape who I am today.

That summer after my mother died, my father would take me to stay with friends of his during the day while he worked. We would go from friend to friend. Sometimes these people would not answer their doors in the morning. This really made my father angry, because it caused him to miss work. One hot humid summer morning we went to two of his friends' houses: one on Waldburg Street (the city block of two-story apartments and houses that we

GONE TOO SOON

lived on); the other in Carver Village in West Savannah...and neither answered their doors. I told my father to give me a key and I could let myself in and out of our house, and play with my friends on Waldburg Street during the day until he got home. My father didn't want to give me a key to the house at that young age (eight years old) but he didn't have much of a choice. Besides, I was very convincing. I don't know why people wouldn't open the door for us--money, my behavior, I really wasn't sure--but my father knew he had to work. So I became a kid with a key, or what is now called a latchkey kid, at eight years old.

School Days

As things began to get back to normal, I returned to Anderson Street Elementary School. Anderson was a classic-looking two-story red brick school with a playground one block long. Things were different now; I found myself daydreaming and not focusing on my schoolwork like I had when my mother was alive. I was not as eager to get home and tell what I learned, or do my homework. I also discovered that my father had not graduated from school. I learned he dropped out of school in the fifth grade. My learning to read at an early age came in handy because I was able to read all of our mail to my father and he really appreciated it. One of many low points of my childhood was the day I came home from school to find my father passed out face down on the floor. This was not long after my mother died, so you can imagine what I was thinking; I thought I had lost my father too. It turned out my father had drunk too much that day. He really took Mom's death hard. My father eventually slowed down on his drinking as time went on, but he still drank heavily on occasion. Sometimes my father's drinking allowed me to get away with doing bad things, but I really wished he wouldn't drink, because he was a different man when he drank. He was a good man, but his alcoholism had a major impact on my life as a child.

Anderson Street Elementary School was an all African-American school in Savannah, Georgia. In the late sixties and early seventies, schools were much different than they are now. Teachers could discipline students by spanking them, and there were very few fights or other problems in the schools. For the most part I did my lessons, but I was never truly focused; I would catch myself

SCHOOL DAYS

daydreaming and thinking about my mother. Because my father didn't have a formal education, I would lie to him about homework and my grades, knowing he didn't understand what was happening in school. I did just enough schoolwork to get by. After school I would let myself in the house, change, and return to the streets. I was supposed to do my homework, but I could always tell my father I did it and he would never check.

My neighborhood was mostly African-American, with a few white families living there too. Most of our neighbors were on welfare or received some other type of government assistance. My father was always too proud to take public assistance even though we were poor and needed it. His pride and desire for independence are part of the reason I am where I am today. My father never accepted a handout. In my neighborhood I would get into whatever all the other boys got into after school; we played sports, hung out, and on occasion we got into trouble stealing and vandalizing property. Most of the bad things I did as a young boy I did because of peer pressure, but I did do a lot of bad things on my own. I am not blaming any of my past behavior I talk about in this book on where and how I grew up. There were good people, and kids in my neighborhood who stayed out of trouble. I made most of those bad choices on my own. I really liked being in school because I knew I had to behave in school and I felt safe there. There were many days when I didn't want school to end.

In 1971, white children were bused to Anderson Street Elementary School. The black kids in my neighborhood had no idea what to expect--I remember all of us running around saying "Polly wants a cracker." The first white friend I ever had was Carl Showalter; he was an athletic kid who was bused in to Anderson. Carl and I would spend hours talking and comparing the differences between blacks and whites. We talked about everything. Carl also taught me a lot about white culture, but mainly we talked about sports. I did not know it at the time, but becoming friends with Carl prepared me for future relationships I would have with white friends and coworkers. Carl taught me that white people were, in many ways, just like us. I realized all white people weren't bad people, and that white people liked a lot of the same things blacks did. I tried to contact Carl while writing this book, but was unsuccessful. I did speak to Carl's father, Carl Sr., and found out Carl Jr. attended the Virginia Military Institute and is now in the construction business, living in Charlotte, North Carolina. I'm sure our relationship at Anderson had a bigger impact on me than it did Carl.

In my old neighborhood on Waldburg Street there were many adults who looked after me, and they told my father what I had been up to while he was at work. While I hated them for telling on me, I now realize if it weren't for some of those nice people I might be dead or in jail. They were just looking out for me and trying to keep me out of trouble. There were the Whiting, Davis, and Brown families. Ms. Nora Whiting had two sons: Aubrey, a handsome bow-legged boy, and Okemi an athletic boy who sometimes got into trouble. I would always be at their house, especially for dinner. Ms. Nora was a great cook. The Davis family moved to Waldburg Street in 1968. There were six children: Jeffrey, Carl, Ronnie, Calvin, Vernon, and Sharon--along with their mother, Ms. Lillian. Carl and I were the same age; we were classmates and best friends. Everyone hung out at the Davis family house. Jeffrey lives here in North Carolina now, and Carl and I are still best friends who still visit each other and stay in touch to this day. Ms. Lillian Davis now lives in a beautiful home on Hilton Head Island; she is still a great cook. The Browns had three children: Michael, Greg, and Derwin. Michael was the oldest, Greg and I were the same age, and Derwin was a newborn. The Browns lived on the west side of town. Mr. Brown and my father would take us to Burger King on Fridays for Whalers (fish sandwiches) and strawberry milkshakes. All of these good people lived on or near Waldburg Street and had

SCHOOL DAYS

a huge impact on me growing up. As a latchkey kid and only child, I was always hanging out at someone's house. My friends' mothers would often feed me, even though most of them struggled financially and couldn't afford to feed an extra mouth; looking back, I really appreciate what they did for me. Those families who took me into their homes when my father worked will never know how much it meant to me.

While my father worked, there were all kinds of things in my neighborhood to get into: there were dice games in the alley; we would steal candy from local stores, play sports, and hang out at houses that sold whiskey by the glass. I was a kid and too young to drink, but I would hang out there to run errands to the store for the grown-ups. In return, they would give me money. There were also fights…and many of them. I was in a fight almost every week. Many of the neighborhood kids would pick fights with me because I was an only child and didn't have a big brother to protect me. Kids with big brothers and large families were mostly left alone by bullies. As you can see, when I got home from Anderson Street Elementary, there was always something to get into, and I got into most of it. I did a lot of things that that I shouldn't have done, and I regret doing them. I lied, I stole, and I vandalized property. I did these things mostly to be accepted by the other boys in the neighborhood. My grades at Anderson were above average because I had some really good teachers. When I was in elementary school, teachers could beat you if you misbehaved. I remember being on the end of my teacher Ms. Stewart's paddle on many days for acting up. I did not know this at the time but the school environment, friends, and teachers at Anderson Street School would prepare me for many tough years ahead. Anderson Street School was my educational foundation.

Meyers Junior High

Just like the white kids had been bused to Anderson Elementary in my neighborhood, it was now time for the black kids to be bused away to school, too. When we received a notice telling us I would be going to Meyers Junior High, there was a lot of anxiety. Kindergarten and elementary school were both in my neighborhood, and we always walked to school. Now I would have to catch the bus and meet a bunch of new kids. I was very nervous, uncomfortable, and a little bit scared. By now I was starting to grow into a young man, I was very handsome and athletic, and started to notice girls…and they started noticing me, too. The one positive I had going into Meyers Junior High was that my friend Carl Davis and some other neighborhood children were going there with me. Unlike Anderson Street Elementary, Meyers' campus was spread out, with several wings on a sprawling piece of land. Students would have to go outside to change classes when the bell rang. It was hard for teachers and principals to keep track of everyone, so cutting class was easy. When we arrived at Meyers, things were different--we were at a white school, and many teachers did not know how to deal with some of the unruly black children; in fact, some of the white female teachers were scared to death. To me it seemed all of the cool kids didn't go to class, didn't do their schoolwork, and gave the teachers a hard time. I knew this behavior was wrong, but I started to act like those kids to gain acceptance. Peer pressure is a very powerful thing when you're young and looking to belong. I stopped doing my schoolwork, I disrespected most of my teachers, and I cut a lot of classes to hang out and smoke cigarettes with people I thought were my friends.

MEYERS JUNIOR HIGH

I flunked out in seventh grade and had to go to summer school to get promoted to eighth grade. This cost my father time and money. When my father asked me why I had to go to summer school I lied to him, saying this was normal. I truly regret doing that, because it cost my father money we didn't have, and lost wages at his job because he had to drive me to summer school.

When I got to the eighth grade, things didn't change--they got worse. Now I started experimenting with marijuana, which along with the alcohol made me sleep in class, and I still wasn't doing any schoolwork. My real friends didn't like the new me, and I was lost, looking for someone to hang out with. As my eighth grade school year went on, I became more and more depressed. The low point of my entire life came one night when I thought about committing suicide. I remember sitting on the side of my bed thinking,

What is there to live for? My mother was gone, my father and I had a difficult relationship, we were poor; on many days I wore the same clothes to school more than once in a week and kids would tease me about it. Things were not going well and I saw no reason to go on. I started to cry really hard and then I fell to my knees and begged God to help me. I was feeling sorry for myself and hopeless. There had to be more to life than this! I was a complete mess.

The Turn-Around

I went to summer school that summer to get promoted to the ninth grade. Again this cost my father money and time he didn't have, but things were different for me now. I vowed to never be in summer school again, and I also vowed to stop causing trouble and causing my father to miss work. It was time I started being responsible and stopped being a knucklehead. Something came over me, and I truly believe it was God answering my prayers for help the night I thought about committing suicide. One of the first successful black men I ever met was a coach at Meyers Junior High Mr. Summerset. Coach Summerset was a handsome thin-mustached black man who drove a Mercedes Benz and came to school well-dressed every day. His shoes were always shined and he made us play golf and do other things in gym class that we were not exposed to. It's ironic, because I am an avid golfer today. Coach Summerset became an inspiration to me.

When I started ninth grade I was determined to put the past behind me, study, and do my schoolwork. I wasted two years of junior high school, but I was determined to change. I went to class, did my schoolwork, and for the most part stayed out of trouble. As my ninth grade year went on I got a girlfriend, played sports, and continued to do my schoolwork. Things were different now I was enjoying school and enjoying life again. I even started to get along better with my father. The highlight of my ninth grade year was the trophy I received for academic excellence in earth science. That small trophy confirmed that I could achieve if I studied and applied myself. I saw my Earth Science teacher Mrs. Irving two years ago at a Kroger's in East Savannah. Mrs. Irving still looked the same,

THE TURN-AROUND

peering over her eyeglasses. I said hello to her and told her how much that Earth Science trophy and the recognition meant to me. At Meyers Junior High I had seen my lowest point in life, yet with the help of God, friends, and family I came through it ready to move on to high school.

Richard Arnold High School

It had been eight years since my mother passed away, and while our lives did go on, I still thought about her a lot. I spent the summer after I left junior high getting ready for high school; my friend Carl and I took summer jobs at M&M supermarket as baggers to earn extra cash. I was excited and scared at the same time about attending high school, because I realized I had three years of school left--then what? Time was really moving now; I was getting closer to becoming an adult.

Richard Arnold High School was a majority African-American school located on Bull Street in Savannah, Georgia. Like Anderson, it was a single-brick two-story building with a lot of character; it was located one block north of the city's main library and one block south of Gotlieb's Bakery, which had the biggest and best doughnuts in town. Richard Arnold was also the only vocational-technical school in Savannah. Arnold offered voc-tech classes like barbering, sheet metal, drafting and design, cosmetology, and food service to name a few. Entering tenth grade, I now understood that I had to get my diploma and make something of myself, but I still wanted to have fun and enjoy myself. This is where I got conflicted. I did enough work to get by, but I also drank alcohol and experimented with drugs. There were times when I would go to class under the influence of alcohol. I also started hanging out with other friends who drank and did drugs too. I quit hanging out with most of my old friends from Waldburg Street. I played junior varsity sports my sophomore year, but I quit playing sports so I could work and earn money for clothes. It was more important for me to look good than play sports. I worked at M&M

RICHARD ARNOLD HIGH SCHOOL

Supermarket, Johnny Harris, and the Pirate's House restaurant. I grew taller and slimmer and became much better-looking. At least, that's what the girls were telling me.

As my sophomore year ended I was mostly focused on my clothes, girls, and getting high. My grades were important, but I didn't do anything extra or try to excel. People started calling me "pretty boy" ("pretty" for short). As I entered the eleventh grade I had no clue what I wanted to do with my life after high school. My eleventh grade year was a blur--in fact I don't remember too much about it. I remember drinking alcohol and continuing to experiment with drugs. One night I drank so much Mad Dog 20/20 (wine) that I could hardly stay awake in school the next day. A good friend of mine, Carolyn Devillers, a pretty girl with big brown eyes, helped me get myself together that morning. She helped me wake up, and let me look at her homework from the night before. Carolyn was a good friend. Looking back on it, I should have been totally embarrassed. While my school grades were enough to get me promoted to the twelfth grade, they weren't nearly good enough to get me into a good college. I always dreamed of being a lawyer or doctor but I did nothing to prepare myself for that type of career. There I was in eleventh grade with one year left in high school, with no plan and mediocre grades.

I mentioned earlier that Arnold High was a voc-tech school. I enrolled in sheet metal my freshman year, but I never really took that class seriously. While some of my classmates were focusing and learning the trade, I was goofing off. Mr Newman, a tall white gentleman with a great sense of humor, was a great teacher and he knew the sheet metal business. In fact, he got several of my classmates jobs after high school. But I was not one of them, because all I did in Mr. Newman's class was goof off. There I was, squandering every opportunity I had.

By the end of the eleventh grade, fear and panic started to set in. I had one last summer to figure out what I was going to do before I graduated from high school. God had blessed me with good looks, good health, and a good brain, but I had done nothing with them. There was emptiness inside me. I felt like a total failure. I quit working at M&M supermarket the summer before my senior year in high school to go to work at the Pirate's House, a famous restaurant near the river in downtown Savannah. There were plenty of good-looking girls working there, and I enjoyed flirting with them. I bused tables that summer and prepared for my last year of school. I bought a lot of nice clothes and got mentally prepared because I knew I had to make some changes. I was seventeen, with very few options for a successful future. I had squandered many opportunities to make something of myself. I even blew a chance to be an extra on the award-winning TV mini-series *Roots* by Alex Haley. The casting directors came to Richard Arnold High during my junior year, looking for dark-skinned black males. I would have been selected if I agreed to cut my afro. I refused to cut my hair, so they passed on me. If you watch the movie, the scene where Kunta Kinte is in chains beside a group of other slaves--those slaves are all my classmates. I regret not cutting my hair for that movie to this day.

Now I needed to focus on my schoolwork, but more importantly, I needed to quit drinking and stay off drugs. My mother had been gone for ten years. If she were here, I wondered, would she be proud of me? Would I be more successful than I was? How would my life have been different in 1978 had my mother lived? It really didn't matter; I had made my bed, and now I had to lie in it. I had made poor choices: I didn't focus in school, and didn't prepare myself for life after high school. This was it. My only goal was to get my high school diploma. I would worry about everything else after that, but I knew I couldn't waste all those years of schooling and not walk across that stage in June 1978.

High School Senior Year

My Second Boyhood Home

As I walked through the doors of Arnold for the first time in my senior year, I had made a transformation. I was taller, better-looking, and extremely well-dressed; the afro was gone, and I had a new sense of confidence. A lot of girls, both seniors and underclassmen, were interested in me. I started the school year doing all the right things. I did above-average schoolwork, worked after school, and really cut back on drinking and drugs for the first few months. I also worked after school at the Pirate's House restaurant. Things were going well. I started dating, and I was happy that things were finally looking up. To celebrate, I started drinking and I started using drugs again. This was disappointing to me, but I didn't care. I was enjoying hanging out with friends and older men from my neighborhood. We drank beer and wine, and smoked pot.

What happened to the focus? What happened to changing and turning my life around? I will tell you it's harder than anyone can imagine, especially when the environment you are in and some of the people around you are into drinking and drugs. I am not blaming anyone for the things I did in high school; I was responsible for my behavior and made bad choices. I know from my experiences how hard it is to stay straight and do what's right. I truly sympathize with today's youth. I realized I had taken a step backward, but I made excuses. I told myself that at least I was working, wearing good clothes, and doing my schoolwork. I made excuses for every bad decision I made during my senior year. Many days I was under the influence of alcohol and marijuana, but was able to hide it from my teachers. The only thing that kept me going was not wanting to disappoint my father and my mother's memory. Every time there was an opportunity to do something really stupid that could possibly had landed me in jail, I would walk away. I credit my father and how he raised me for doing this. Even though he had to work, he always taught me to do what's right. I would not be where I am today if I'd had any type of trouble with the law.

So I went on. Senior year in high school was fun. There were events only for seniors: dances, trips, boat rides…we had to take pictures for our yearbook, and we selected senior superlatives. I was voted most talented in our senior yearbook, which I still have and I still look at on occasion. It started to set in that my senior year was half over and soon I would be a graduate, and would have to go out into the real world.

As my senior prom approached, I started to calculate who I wanted to take. There were several girls who wanted me to ask them, but I thought I was so cool that I could choose a date at the very last minute. I was also trying to be the guy who walked in with the prettiest girl. As the prom got closer I started asking girls out only to find out that all the girls I wanted to take had already accepted dates from other guys. I was very disappointed, there were girls still available for the prom, but my ego wouldn't let me ask a girl that I

HIGH SCHOOL SENIOR YEAR

thought was unpopular to the prom, so I stayed at home.

I remember wondering what my classmates were doing at the prom that night. On my prom night I was out drinking beer with some older guys from my neighborhood. The next school day I recall all my friends talking about the prom and how much fun they had. All I could do was listen with envy. I regret missing my senior prom to this day. What should have been a special night with a special young lady never happened because of my ego. When we returned to school after the prom, we had very little time left before graduation. Rehearsals and other administrative events filled our days, right up to graduation.

I was selected to be the master of ceremonies for our graduation and it was quite an honor. There were many other seniors much more deserving, but I was articulate, good-looking, and I had a deep strong voice. Today when I speak at schools, I always tell the children you will never forget your high school graduation day. It is the culmination of twelve years of sacrifice and hard work. I will never forget my graduation night. It was a warm summer day June 4 1978. I woke up that morning with butterflies in my stomach. I had strange feelings of joy, accomplishment, and fear. I remember talking to my father that morning. Our relationship really got better over the years as I started to become a man. I realized many of the things he taught me were not to make my life miserable, but to set me up for success. If only I had listened and applied some of his teachings earlier in life, I would have been heading off to college that fall instead of wondering what my next move would be. My father was old school; he never hugged me or told me he loved me. He grew up in a time when men didn't show that kind of affection toward their sons. I don't recall my father telling me he was proud of me for graduating; it was what I was supposed to do.

Even though I never heard the words, I knew he loved me and I knew he was proud. As the moments grew closer for me to graduate, I got more nervous. Not only did I have to graduate I had to MC the event. I was a nervous wreck! By the time graduation came around I had calmed down and was ready to go. Ready to do this! The commencement exercises were at five o' clock, I had to be there at three o' clock. As we rehearsed at the Savannah Civic Center, I was finally going to graduate from high school. Twelve years of school were almost over. I did a pretty good job with my portion of the graduation ceremony. As I walked across the stage, I will never forget the feelings I had, feelings of pride and accomplishment. It was a wonderful night--one I will never forget. I was a high school graduate.

You're in the Army Now

Babylon Iraq 2003

After high school I continued working at the Pirate's House restaurant. I got promoted from a busboy to a waiter. Waiters got paid mostly in tips, and because the Pirate's House was a tourist attraction, the patrons who ate there tipped really well. I was out of high school, living at home and waiting tables at a restaurant. I always thought I would go to college, but we couldn't afford it and I didn't get good enough grades to be offered a scholarship. I made pretty good money because I was always polite to the people I served, and I told my customers about places and other nice restaurants to visit in Savannah. I also started dating some of the waitresses and other staff members. I worked at the Pirate's House for a few months after high school, but I quickly got bored. I remember thinking, *There has to be something better than this.* My friend Carl's brother Jeffrey went in the Army in 1977 and returned to be stationed at Fort Stewart, Georgia, which was forty-three miles from Savannah.

Jeffrey would come home on weekends in his uniform, driving his new car. We all thought this was very cool. I remember thinking I should go into the Army myself. I talked to Carl about it, but he was not interested in going at the time. I talked to my father and he didn't seem too thrilled about my joining the Army, either.

As I lay in my bedroom looking at the mirrored walls and the Hotel California mural I had painted on my wall, I thought about my future--there had to be something better than waiting tables. Tomorrow I would go to see the Army recruiters. On a hot humid morning in June 1978 I went to the recruiter's office downtown and walked through the door. My life would change that day forever!

The recruiter was a tall black sergeant who looked really good in his uniform. He welcomed me in and pulled my ASVAB (test) scores. These were the results from the military entry test I had taken while I was in high school. As he started telling me which jobs I qualified for, I quickly realized I should have taken those military tests more seriously. I was not qualified for many of the jobs I wanted to do in the military because my test scores weren't high enough. When I took those tests in high school I had no intention of joining the Army, so I basically blew off those tests, and I didn't even finish them.

However, I did well enough to get in the Army--I just didn't qualify for some of the more technical jobs. Logistics was the most appealing job the recruiter had available and I was ready to leave Savannah, so I signed up. I remember walking home from the recruiter's office stunned. I had done it; I'd signed up to join the United States Army.

I was leaving for Fort Jackson, South Carolina in two weeks to take a physical and process into the military. If that went well, I would be going to basic combat training in Jan 1979. I boarded a bus to Columbia, South Carolina to take a military physical and be sworn in to the military. There were dozens of us getting poked and prodded by military doctors. If there was something medically wrong with you, those doctors were going to find it. Many were not allowed to join the Army because of medical conditions they had.

After all the tests and interviews were complete, we were all taken into a room where we raised our right hands and took an oath to protect and defend the United States of America. We were now soldiers! When I returned from my military physical and processing, I was officially in the Army with a reporting date for basic combat training of Jan 23, 1979.

I had a little over five months in Savannah before I left home for good. I was excited and scared at the same time--what had I done? I wanted to leave home, but there was a part of me that wondered… had I made the right decision? Seeing my friend Jeffrey come home in his uniform was one thing; my being in a uniform was another. There was excitement and doubt. I spent those five months working at the Pirate's House and dating a chocolate-skinned girl named Florence. Florence looked like a model; she had perfect skin. I also started to feel a little guilty about leaving my father. He had been there for me when my mom died and now I was leaving him at home alone. I really struggled with this. The months flew by; before I knew it I had a few weeks left before I reported for basic training.

You can never prepare for joining the military. I worked out some while I was at home so I would be in decent shape when I arrived at basic. But other than that I had no idea what to expect. As the days started to get closer to my departure, I realized that my life was going to change forever. I was going away, into the Army. I was going to be a real man. My last night in Savannah was spent with Florence on the beach. It was a cold clear night in January--in fact it was too cold to be on the beach, but I knew it would be a while before I would be able to visit the beach again. We sat and talked as the tides came in, and I knew I had only hours left as a civilian. The next day--Jan 23, 1979--my father took me to the Greyhound bus station. He gave me the usual warnings about behaving and avoiding the stockade (Army jail). We shook hands and I boarded the bus for what turned out to be one of the decisions that defined and forever changed my life.

Basic Training

When the bus pulled up to Fort Jackson, South Carolina where basic training was being conducted, I started to hear loud noises that sounded like voices and chaos. As we got closer, the noises got louder; the next thing I knew, a drill sergeant was beating on the bus window, yelling for us to get off the bus. As soon as we got off the bus, the drill sergeant made us do jumping jacks and push-ups until exhaustion. What in the world had I gotten myself into?

As I did those jumping jacks and push-ups on the cold January ground in South Carolina, I just knew I had made a mistake. The recruiter told me I could learn a trade, get money for college, and travel the world--but he didn't mention anything about doing exercise and being yelled at in the cold! The drill sergeant was a tall muscular black man with a booming voice. "Look at all you maggots; you came here to ruin my Army," he said. "Well, I'm not going to let that happen. I'm going to make you quit." The drill sergeant said, "Does anyone want to quit now?" As I stood there sweating in the winter cold from the physical training (PT), I did think about quitting for a minute there. Maybe the Army wasn't for me. I could always go back home and find a job. But something hit me. I realized I could not go back home after one day because someone yelled at me and made me do push-ups; I couldn't go back to Waldburg Street as a failure--but more importantly, I could not let my father down. I could not face him…especially if I quit.

I told myself the only way I was going home was if the Army told me they did not want me. I would not quit, no matter how hard it got--and believe me, it got very hard. Waking up every morning at

0330, then going outside to do physical training in freezing weather, was tough on all of us. After we did physical training, we would train all day. The drill sergeants were trying to turn teenage civilians into soldiers in eight weeks. This was no easy task. My drill sergeants' last names were Chambers and Alvin. Their first names were Drill Sergeant. Both were black males, both were tough, and both were physically fit; Chambers was six feet tall and stood erect like he owned the world. Alvin was about six feet four inches tall and walked with a certain swagger. Whenever we marched by, women always paid a lot of attention to Alvin. These two men and my classmates were the only family I had for the next eight weeks. By the way, my first name became "trainee"--so did all the other recruits' first names.

So we went on day after day, week after week...marching, running, shooting, and training. The more I trained, the better I became at soldiering. Everything was going great until one evening in the barracks. There was a trainee named Bodley from Chicago. He was a loudmouth know-it-all, and nobody liked him. He would regularly bully trainees in the barracks after the drill sergeants left for the night. This night he came up to me wanting to pick a fight, and I was in no mood for it. We started fighting, and pretty soon it looked like a scene out of a movie--trainees yelling, furniture moving, things breaking...it was ugly! The next thing I knew, a hand was grabbing me by my shirt behind my neck. It was Drill Sergeant Chambers, and he was not happy.

He took both of us to his office and said he was going to send both of us home. After four weeks of hard training, I had thrown it all away because I wasn't smart or disciplined enough to walk away from a fight. How could I be so stupid? When Drill Sergeant Chambers called me into his office, I started to cry. I told him this was not the way I wanted to go home--for something as stupid as fighting. After all, I'd joined the Army to get away from all that. I

BASIC TRAINING

promised him that if he gave me another chance I would prove to him that I could be a soldier. I begged him. As I stood there awaiting his verdict, I realized this must be what it was like to stand in front of a judge.

When Drill Sergeant Chambers began to speak, I was extremely nervous. He said, "Boy, I'm going to let you stay, but if you get into any more trouble I will send your butt home so quick you won't know what hit you." Whew, I had dodged a bullet and gotten a second chance to stay in the Army.

After the fight with Private Bodley, I knew I could not afford to mess up again. From that point on I did everything my drill sergeants told me to do, and I studied hard to become a good soldier. I graduated from basic combat training in March 1979 with a certificate for superior performance. This was the first time I had achieved anything as an adult. I was lean, mean, strong, and handsome. I had completed the toughest challenge in my life. I wished my father could have come to the graduation. As my classmates and I waited for our orders to our next assignment, I had no idea what was in store for me, but I knew whatever was waiting for me after finishing basic training I was ready.

When my name was called, I got my orders to report to Fort Lee, Virginia for Advanced Individual Training (AIT). This training would prepare me to do the job that I would perform daily in the Army. I would be trained as a Material Handling and Storage Specialist, which was a supply worker with a focus on warehousing and forklift driving. I probably could have gotten a better military specialty, but I was in such a rush to leave Savannah that I hadn't done much research. AIT was nothing like basic training. We had more freedom, we didn't work nights, and we had most weekends free. We went to school every day to learn how the Army handled and stored all the equipment in its inventory. We marched and sang songs to and from school every day. AIT was fun, but to this day I cannot tell you the names of any of my instructors there. They clearly did not make an impact on me like Drill Sergeants Chambers and Alvin did. After eight weeks I was graduating again, this time from AIT. I had completed all my training. Now I was a soldier and was ready to report to my first duty station as a permanent party soldier.

Private Drayton Reporting for Duty

Fort Stewart, Georgia 1979

I received orders for Fort Stewart, Georgia which is forty-three miles from Savannah where I grew up--the same base my friend Jeffrey was stationed at when he joined the Army. Part of me was excited to be returning home, and part of me wasn't. I took a week's vacation--or as we called in the Army, leave--before I reported to Fort Stewart. I went back to Savannah to visit my father and see some of my old high school and neighborhood friends. After spending a week at home I was glad I had joined the Army. Most of my friends were at home doing the same old things they had been doing before I left. I had made the right decision to join the Army.

I reported to Fort Stewart in early June 1979 to the 632nd Maintenance Company. As I drove up to the pretty brick building with the manicured lawn, I did not know what to expect. I heard that permanent party was different from basic training and AIT and I was about to find out. I opened the door of the 632nd orderly room and announced, "Private Drayton reporting for duty." Private E-1 is the lowest rank you can hold in the entire US Army. You are not supposed to know anything, not supposed to talk, and definitely not supposed to have an opinion about anything related to the military. After all, you are new to the military and you are just completing your training. Well, no one told me that. I reported to my first duty station full of confidence and opinions.

My first platoon sergeant SFC (E-7) Whitehead, a chain-smoking tall slender black man and Viet Nam veteran, came to pick me up from the company headquarters. "Where are you from?" he said. When I told him Savannah, he gave me a stern look and said, "Boy, you are going to be trouble, you are too close to home."

My reply was, "No, Sergeant--I will be fine."

When I showed up at the warehouse, all my coworkers came to greet me. There were blacks and whites, women and men. This was my first job in the Army. I was responsible for processing and storing incoming repair parts. The work was really easy and not very challenging, but I did have a lot of fun with my coworkers, and I really liked working for SFC Whitehead.

My platoon leader was a black female lieutenant named Stringield. She was attractive, with a nice figure and a distinctive raspy voice. I had a crush on her. I kept my nose clean and my uniform very sharp, and did my job. When you do this, people notice you. I was promoted to E-2 and E-3 after serving only nine months in the Army. In November 1979 the 632nd needed a mail clerk and selected me because of my uniform appearance and my work ethic. This was a promotion somewhat, because even though I wasn't doing my military job I was able to work great hours and I never had to work in the cold or heat again. My job consisted of going to the Fort Stewart post office to pick up the mail for all 200 people in my unit, then bring it back, sort it out, and issue it to the soldiers during mail call. This included paychecks, which came twice a month. This was before direct deposit. It was a very important job.

I made some good friends at Ft. Stewart, too: Eddie Harris, a tall light-skinned black guy from Florida; and Ronald Thomas (Ice T) another brother from Florida. T had a gold tooth and a brand-new car, and was really smooth. I also worked with Smalls, a muscular white guy from Biddeford Poole, Maine. Smalls and I were the two mail clerks in the unit. We would take off early and go hang out and listen to music. On many weekends I would go home to Savannah to hang out with my friends Carl Davis and Donald Bryant. Life was good. I was nineteen years old, had steady employment, and even though I was stationed forty-three miles from home, I still had left home and had accomplished something. My first assignment at Fort Stewart was a good start to my military career. I was learning responsibility and becoming independent.

Germany

I returned one day with the mail to find SFC Whitehead and some others in the headquarters looking at me with a wry grin and laughing. I asked them what the matter was. They smiled and said, "Do you think you'll like Germany?"

I replied, "I don't know--why?"

SFC Whitehead looked at me and said, "Because that's where you're going!"

I stood there shocked and terrified...Germany? Everyone in the headquarters was laughing. It was as if they enjoyed telling the boy from Savannah, the boy who went home on most weekends, that his homesteading was over.

They really enjoyed giving me that news. I quickly pulled myself together and played it off like it was no big deal. Oh, but it was a big deal. This would be my first time overseas--but more importantly, this would be the first time I would be away from the East Coast. This was a huge, life-changing event. SFC Whitehead gave me my orders. I was to report to Frankfurt, Germany's 21st Replacement Detachment, in September 1980. I had eight months to prepare for my new assignment in a foreign country on the other side of the world. I was not happy. When I told my father the news, he was not too excited about it. Other than basic training and AIT, I had never been away from my father longer than a few months. Plus I was still helping him with things around the house, and reading and

GERMANY

interpreting his mail. There was also a feeling of guilt, because after all, I really joined the Army to get away from my father. But after being stationed at Fort Stewart I really enjoyed being home, and my father and I got along much better once I returned from basic training. I think he had a certain amount of respect for me because I had become a soldier.

I continued to do my mail clerk duties in the 632nd while I prepared for my overseas assignment in Germany. I got promoted to E-4 three months before I left for Germany. I out processed from the 632nd in late August said goodbye to all my friends and coworkers, and took two weeks' leave (vacation) before I departed. I spent two weeks with my father and friends, hanging out and doing things around the house. As the day to leave got closer, I really started to appreciate my father and being home. Everything I wanted to get away from were now the things I wanted to remain close to. I spent the last night in Savannah with my girl Florence, and once again we went to Savannah Beach and looked at the stars. Tomorrow I would be on a plane for Germany. My father took me to the airport, we said our goodbyes, and I was off to start a new adventure.

On the plane ride over I met a pretty girl named Sonya. Sonya had a curly afro and she wore glasses. I noticed her laughing at me in the airport so I approached her to find out what was so funny? Come to find out I had on mismatched socks. Sonya was a female soldier and was heading to Germany too. We sat together and talked all the way over to Germany, enjoying each other's company.

It was great to have someone to talk to, which made the seven-hour flight go by very fast. As the plane made its approach into Frankfurt, I remember looking down over the city in amazement. This was my first time out of the United States. We were met by a sergeant from the 21st Replacement Detachment, which is a place where soldiers go to wait for their next assignment in Germany. The 21st

sent soldiers to units throughout Germany to replace soldiers who had finished their overseas assignments and were returning to the States. We in-processed, and waited around in Frankfurt for a few days for our assignments. Sonya and I hung out talked and dined together while we waited. Sonya got her assignment first; she was headed to a town called Schwabisch-Gmund, which was east of Stuttgart. I had known Sonya for only a week, but I really liked her, and part of me was wishing we could be stationed close together. We hugged and said our goodbyes.

I continued to wait for my assignment. As I waited around the 21st Replacement Detachment, it really began to get boring. I was tired of just sitting around, and I wanted to get to my assignment. Finally, after about a week, I was called in and told where I was going to go. I would be assigned to Hanau, which was 21 km away from Frankfurt. I would be assigned to the 3rd/59th Air Defense Artillery Battalion.

I held the rank of E-4 when I arrived at the 3/59. I recall signing in, and everyone walking by the office to check me out and see who I was. Every military organization had a logistics hub assigned to it. That logistics hub was where I would be working in the 3/59th.

After in-processing, I was introduced to my new platoon sergeant, and some of my coworkers. This was very different from what I had experienced being stationed at Fort Stewart. When you're stationed in the United States there are many things to do, everyone speaks the same language, and people tend to stick to themselves and do their own thing. Being assigned in Germany, there were many cultural differences. There were huge language barriers, especially for new soldiers, and people tended to form groups and cliques to make up for being so far away from home.

So, as you can imagine, being a new person assigned to a new unit

GERMANY

could be very hard. I started to get to know my coworkers and befriend some of them. I started learning the ropes and how things worked being assigned overseas. I also learned the differences between Germans and Americans. When I first got to Germany I was extremely homesick. The weather was cold, skies were always grey, rarely did the sun come out, and I didn't have any friends. I didn't have a car, and I missed my father and my old friends back home. Anyone who has ever served in the military and has gone away on their first overseas assignment has probably felt the same way. But I still felt very alone. I went to the post-locator to try to find Sonya. I wrote her a letter and was very surprised to hear that Sonya was happy to hear from me and wanted me to come up for a visit.

So after my first week of German head start, which is a course to that teaches you how to speak German, German culture, and how to travel using the German transportation systems, I planned a trip to see Sonya. I purchased a train ticket to Schwabisch- Gmund. It was my first time on the train alone, and it was really exciting. Schwabisch-Gmund was in the southern part of Germany, which is rich in culture, and the countryside was very beautiful. When I got there, Sonya was waiting for me at the train station; we went to my hotel, where we caught up on what each other had been doing. We went to a dance that night, and I returned to Hanau the following day--it was a great trip for me. I suddenly became more confident and felt better because I knew how to travel and use the German train system, and I had a friend in country that I could talk to, and a place to visit.

So things were looking up. I really liked my job in Germany. I worked in a warehouse at first, pulling and storing repair parts for major end items. The end items were radars that guarded Germany against missiles from the Soviet Union. In the early 1980s, the biggest threat to the US military and its allies was still the old Iron

Curtain, which we called the Soviet Union. Everything on the job was fine, but there was not very much to do in the afternoons when we got off from work. So I started to play sports like football, basketball, and softball to pass the time. I also met some very colorful characters over in Germany.

There was Scooby (Scoob), a tall black well-dressed, brother from Houston, Texas. Scooby's whole thing was about having fun, dating German girls, and going to clubs. So as you can imagine, whenever I joined Scoob on one of his trips to Frankfurt--or should I say, our trips to Frankfurt—it was always a good time. We would dance and hang out, sometimes till two or three o'clock in the morning. Then there was Big Lewis (Lew), a heavyset brother from Chicago with a big gap-toothed smile and a great sense of style. Lew didn't like to go out much. Lewis would just stay in the barracks, listen to music, and cook. It was always great to hang out with Lew, because he was a contrast to Scooby, who always wanted to party. Some evenings and weekends I would hang out with Lew; we would just sit in the barracks, listen to music, and prepare gourmet meals, if that's what you want to call them.

There were many other characters in Germany, from all backgrounds and races, but Lew and Scooby were two of my closest friends while I was stationed there. Together, we three had a lot of fun. We partied hard, dated German girls, and drank a lot of German beer on the weekends. This was our routine, but quite frankly for me it began to get boring. The times when I was alone I often wondered, *What am I doing? Why am I now in the military with all these opportunities, yet I'm still hanging out, drinking, and doing some of the same things I did when I was in high school?*

I really wrestled with this. Some weekends I would take trips to other parts of Germany just to get away from the mundane things I was doing in Hanau. On most weekends I just stayed there in

GERMANY

Hanau hanging out with my friends. Occasionally I would meet up with a German girl and spend the weekend at her place, but dating German women was very hard. There were many cultural differences, plus you usually had to travel to link up with them.

Even though I didn't always make the best use of my time when I was off work, I did very well on the job in the 3/59th. When I got to Germany I was working in a warehouse where it was very cold and the work was mundane and not very rewarding. But because of the way I conducted myself on the job, and my appearance, I was promoted to stock control, which put me inside where it was warm, and also exposed me to my first computer-related job. My job was to keypunch data into a large computer to track and manage the items that were in the warehouse, where I used to work. I got to work on my first computer in 1980. I also was approached about becoming a noncommissioned officer. The opportunity to work on computers and to become a noncommissioned officer came my way because I always conducted myself like a professional, and had a good appearance. Day in and day out I continued to do my job and hang out with my friends on the weekends. I started to get bored with that, too. There had to be more to life, to the military, and to Germany than what I was doing.

Private Johnson

It was a normal workday we had just finished physical training. We grabbed some breakfast and were walking to work. That's when I saw her, one of the prettiest girls I had ever seen. She was walking back toward the barracks. She had caramel skin, long hair with blonde streaks in it, and the most beautiful eyes I had ever seen. Her beauty stopped me in my tracks. When we got to work I started to ask questions about her and was told that she had just gotten there, and was assigned to our organization, the 3/59th. I also told myself that many men would be interested in her. So I was not going to push or be aggressive. As a matter of fact, I decided to ignore her and not pursue her at all. Her name was Private Lila Johnson. She was beautiful, and everyone wanted to date her. So for several months, I continued to hang out with my friends, dating German girls and partying at the clubs. One Friday evening, I had barracks duty called CQ, which was an acronym for "charge of quarters." When you were on CQ duty you were responsible for sitting at a desk in the barracks and maintaining order for a 24-hour period. You had to stay up all night.

I did not know it at the time, but this night of CQ duty would change my life forever. Life is strange sometimes—when you first lay eyes on someone, you never know how your lives will be changed or intertwined. While on CQ that night I was sitting at my desk, getting ready to put on a stocking cap to maintain the waves in my hair. This was something most black men did to achieve a certain wavy look by pressing their hair down with a woman's stocking. As I put the stocking cap on I noticed my last stocking cap had a hole in it. I knocked on the door behind the CQ desk, Private Johnson

PRIVATE JOHNSON

answered. I asked her if she had a spare stocking I could use as cap? Private Johnson found one of her stockings and gave it to me; she then came out to the desk and sat with me. We started talking for a while and before we knew it, the sun was coming up. We had stayed up and talked all night long. It had been a long time since I had that long a conversation with a female.

I really liked her, so I asked her to go out with me that Saturday to thank her for sitting up with me, and keeping my company all night. Lila agreed to go out with me. We went to downtown Hanau to do some shopping and sightseeing, and to enjoy a nice German meal. We had a wonderful time, and we hit it off quite well. Before we knew it, we were dating each other exclusively, and spending a lot of time together. I moved out of the barracks and into a house with a coworker named Bradley and his wife. Lila would come over and visit me. This arrangement didn't work out too well, because as we all know there can be only one man of the house. So after several months, I moved back into the barracks. A few months later, Lila became pregnant with our first child. I was twenty-one years old, and to be honest with you, quite afraid of becoming a father, but it was a challenge that I would embrace and I vowed to be there for my child. I had seen so many young women back home raising children by themselves. I felt I needed to be there for my firstborn child.

We found a nice little apartment off-base and moved in right away. It was a three-story attic apartment with a small kitchen, and a beautiful view of downtown Erlenese. But most of all it was home. It was my first place of my own. Lila and I would live together in that apartment throughout her pregnancy, as we anxiously awaited the birth of our child.

Life was good then, even though neither one of us knew what to expect. We loved each other and both of us were excited about having a baby. We had great memories in our first apartment, we had friends over on holidays, and we had cookouts and so many other great memories.

My relationship with Lila really changed me for the better--it straightened me out. I stopped hanging out, smoking, and drinking with my friends, and I became more responsible. Lila and I were very happy when we moved off base into our apartment. We both got paid housing allowances and were both making decent money while we were stationed in Germany. I had no idea when I first laid eyes on her that she would be the mother of my first child. That nine months flew by as we eagerly awaited the birth of our child.

On February 13, 1982 I became a father for the first time. This was a life-changing event for me because I knew that for the rest of her life, this beautiful little girl would be depending on me to guide and protect her. We named her Tiffanie. I had to make some major changes and I had to make them now. Because we weren't married, Lila and I departed Germany at different times; she got assigned to a base in Colorado and I got assigned to a base in Virginia. I got to spend only a few months with my little girl while we were in Germany, but those were some of the most joyous months of my life.

In October of 1982, Lila and I got married and moved to Virginia. Virginia is where our second child was born, another beautiful little girl we named Brittny.

I was stationed at Fort Eustis, Virginia from 1982 to 1985, which included a one-year tour in South Korea. I was twenty-five years old with a wife and two children, and not a lot of direction or experience. I was an E4 in the Army, which didn't pay a lot of money, so I had to do side jobs to make ends meet, because we didn't want to put our children in day care at an early age. I was still very young and I had issues with discipline. There were times when I was selfish and hung out with my friends when I should have been home with my family.

I finally got promoted to sergeant in 1985, but we still needed extra money to pay the bills and pay for extras we needed for our kids. I drove a pizza truck concession at night to make ends meet. This was a tough job, because I had to work late hours at night, and be ready to perform my military duties early the next morning. I worked those two jobs for almost a year, until I received orders to go to Korea. My tour in Korea was unaccompanied, which meant Lila and the girls would stay in Virginia while I served my one-year tour in Korea.

I missed the first year of Brittny's life because of that Korean tour, but that is common in the military. I wasn't the only soldier separated from his family. Thousands of soldiers did this every year. Deployments are part of the military. Compared to what our troops are facing today, I had it easy. Being separated from my family also put a strain on our marriage. We were very young and had never been separated. Lila and I almost got divorced in 1986. This was what it was like for many military families. I am so glad we worked through everything and stayed together. We have been married for thirty years.

While stationed in Korea. I got another promotion to Staff Sergeant E6. Being a staff sergeant at such a young age (twenty-six) brought our family more money, and me a lot more respect from my peers and subordinates. I had figured out how to get promoted in the military: hard work and dedication, education, and punctuality were crucial to earning respect and being looked at for jobs with increased responsibility. This formula would help me get promoted all the way to the top enlisted rank of Sergeant Major E-9.

When I returned from Korea I was assigned to Fort Bragg, North Carolina, home of the airborne. This assignment would change my life forever, and allow me to serve in one of the most elite military organizations in the world.

From 1986 through 2004 I was assigned to Fort Bragg, North Carolina, where I served in the First Corps Support Command, and the Army's elite Delta Force. I graduated from The US Army Airborne School and numerous other military schools and academies. I also went from the rank of Staff Sergeant E-6 to Sergeant Major E-9 during that period. I was a senior logistician, and held several high-profile positions in operations. I was fortunate enough to travel all over the world, spending as many as 200 days a year on the road. Some of the deployments and assignments at Fort Bragg exposed me to events, situations, and opportunities that most Americans will never experience. They also made me wiser and better-prepared to deal with business, family, and life in general. I owe a lot to the military. I owe more to the men and women of Delta, many of whom gave me opportunities they didn't have to give me.

In 2004, I retired from the military as a sergeant major. I received the Legion of Merit, the military's fifth-highest award, and had a wonderful retirement ceremony, which was attended by my peers, friends, and family. Since my retirement I have been an analyst for a major corporation, a broadcaster and station manager for a local radio station, a school teacher, a senior Department of Defense civilian, and I currently own my own company--Drayton Communications. My wife and I live in a gated golf course community in eastern North Carolina. It has been forty-two years since my mother's funeral. As I reflect back on all that has happened, I know that I have been truly blessed and fortunate to have accomplished what I have and to live the way I do. I had a lot of help from a lot of people. There are too many to name them all.

PRIVATE JOHNSON

As you can see, enlisting in the Army was a great decision. I had a stellar military career, met my beautiful wife, had two wonderful children, and learned lessons no college or university could have taught me. I also learned how to be disciplined, hard-working, and honest. I owe much of what I have accomplished to the decision to visit that recruiter back in 1978. I went into the Army a mess, and retired from the Army as a soldier.

Considering where I grew up, I could have easily been a statistic and wound up in prison or a victim of street violence. Education and the military prepared me and provided structure and discipline. Today, African-American males are almost extinct when it comes to relevance and what we contribute to society. Our young men are failing in school, filling the prisons, and fathering children way too early in life. I wrote this book to help guide the many troubled black youth that lack direction and need help finding their talent and achieving success in their own lives.

Saddam Hussein's Palace Iraq

Essentials for Success

With Vice President Biden 2006

In the chapters to follow I would like to share with you my recipes and my blueprint for success as an African-American. As I write this, I realize we have a black president. This is something I am truly proud of. However, there are too many young African-Americans who are not following our president's example in regard to education, conduct, responsibility, and appearance. If we are to succeed in society we have to make some drastic changes. As you turn the pages, take notes--use a highlighter do whatever it takes to retain the information in this book and you too can succeed while black.

Education, Education, Education

If you visit an infant ward at a hospital, you will see several babies waiting to go home with their parents. At that point in their lives, all of those babies are equal, and they all have a chance at success in life, but who that child goes home with has everything to do with their odds of achieving success. Some children are almost doomed from the time they leave the hospital because of the situations they will be brought into. Add to that the obstacles black children face in public schools; in most cases the deck is definitely stacked against most African-American youth. Education is a way out of any situation you may face in life; throughout history many African-Americans have improved their situation in life through receiving an education. An education can be formal, through book learning; or an education can be learning through other sources like on-the-job training, vocational school, and life experiences. What I am talking about now is a formal education, which is something that all young African-Americans have the opportunity to achieve in America today. Over 750 of our ancestors died during the civil rights movement fighting for equality and the right to receive the same opportunities as everyone else in America. Some young African-Americans today seem to have forgotten all those before us who have sacrificed.

As a substitute schoolteacher in the North Carolina school system, I have seen a pattern of disrespect and outright disdain for higher learning. How did we get here? Some people blame rap music, some blame television, and some blame current society as a whole. We live in times now when everything is achieved very quickly; there are young millionaires everywhere. Some have achieved their wealth through the entertainment industry and many others, specifically minorities, have achieved their wealth through athletics--but that is a small percentage of African-Americans.

The majority of African-Americans will not and cannot become successful through the entertainment or sports industry. This is why an education is so important. I am a product of the inner-city school system. I went to public schools my whole life. There are many distractions in the public school system. There are many kids who have issues at home, live in poverty, live with single parents who work, and there are cases where some children are homeless. All of these factors can affect you as an individual in the classroom. School can be like a sanctuary, a place where for several hours a day you can learn and grow. I am going to talk about how to focus, and how to achieve good grades in school. Some of the things I'm going to talk about may seem simple, but if you apply them, they will help you to focus, make better grades, and thrive in any classroom.

Punctuality

The first thing I want to talk about is punctuality, which simply means being on time for not only school but for everything in your life for the rest of your life. If you're on time for school, work, social events, and everything else, your life will become so much easier. I can't stress how important punctuality is. This is a major issue for many Americans of all races, but especially African-Americans. We are usually late for everything. Our tardiness has become the source of jokes for many stand-up comedians. Why is being on time so important? Being on time is important because it is essential for preparation and sets the stage for success. It can be the difference between failure and success, having a bad day or a great day. I will give you an example: when you oversleep, and you are late for school, your day usually starts out pretty rough. You don't have the time to prepare yourself or your schoolwork; you may forget and leave something at home which puts you behind and starts you off on the wrong path for the entire day.

The same is true when you arrive late for work. You will normally have an encounter with your supervisor or your coworkers, and again start off your day in a negative atmosphere. Now let's reverse this and say you arrive at school on time. You get up early; you've gotten all of your books and assignments together; you've had a good breakfast and you are in class a few minutes early. I think we can all agree this type of day always goes better than the former.

I owe a large portion of my success to being punctual, because I am always on time for everything. As a matter of fact, I am usually early for everything. If you don't believe what I'm telling you, I encourage you to try being ten minutes early for everything for the rest of your life, and you will quickly see a change in your life. That's right--something as simple as being ten minutes early for everything can set you apart from others. It shows that you're responsible, that you want to be there, and it shows your teachers and supervisors that you are willing and ready to go to work. It's that simple: punctuality sets the stage for success. Simply put, it is hard to achieve or be good at anything in life if you don't show up on time for it.

Attitude

Being on time is important, but if you arrive early with a poor attitude, you may as well have not showed up at all. Attitude is arguably the most important behavior characteristic there is. A great attitude toward school, work, and life can propel you to success or get you out of any crisis you may encounter. A poor attitude can cause you problems and setbacks in all aspects of your life.

I'm going to give you a few examples. If you come to school or work every day with a frown on your face, a nasty disposition, and a negative attitude, your classmates and coworkers will more than likely stay away from you. Your teachers and supervisors will more than likely not help you or give you promotions on your job. All of us have displayed a bad attitude at some point in our lives--no one's perfect--but if you are displaying a bad attitude all the time, you have a problem and your life is going to be very stressful and probably not very productive.

Bad attitudes come from negativity and a lack of discipline. Negativity can be in the home, it can come from family, friends, coworkers and supervisors. Negativity can also come from a lack of understanding of a particular issue. We must have patience and tolerance with others to be successful. Try to understand someone else's point of view. This is why I always tell young people: Surround yourself with positive people, and you will have a positive outlook on life. Surround yourself with negative people, and you will have a negative outlook on life and a poor attitude toward life.

There is a saying that when you smile, the world smiles with you. This saying is very true. A simple smile can open many doors for you; a great attitude can also open many doors for you. Horrible attitudes are amongst the biggest behavior issues I see with young people today. You should make an effort to smile and be polite to everyone you come in contact with. You never know who you may need help from later in life. Many of the people we meet early on will usually play some important role in our lives down the road. Having a positive attitude and being polite will change your life. I can guarantee that your life will change if you have a positive attitude.

Principles of Success

While there are many principles of success, I would like to focus on five of them. These five principles of success I believe to be the foundation of success in school, in the workplace, and in life as a whole. When we define success, we are talking about a positive outcome, which does not necessarily always mean wealth and fame. The principles of success I'm going to talk about are commitment, character, integrity, discipline, and work ethic. We will focus on these principles, because for African-Americans--and all young people becoming adults--they are the foundation for success. They are the principles that will give you the blueprint to become successful for the rest of your life. We will look at each one of these principles of success separately.

Discipline

Discipline comes from the word disciple, which means to teach. Discipline is something you do for someone, not to them. Often when we think of the word discipline we think of punishment, or we think of being dealt with severely for something we did wrong. We're going to look at the word discipline in a different light. Being disciplined can almost certainly guarantee you success in life. Children who are undisciplined usually have a hard time adapting and surviving in the world when they become adults, because this world is governed by rules and structure. We would not have as many institutions, structures, and laws that govern us today if our ancestors hadn't had discipline. This is why discipline is so important for young children to learn at an early age.

Discipline, routines, and structure at an early age are very important for parents to provide for their children. Once a child understands structure and routine, things will more easily fall into place, and your child will adapt to life outside of his or her household more easily. For example, in school you are provided a schedule of a lesson plan and a series of events each day that you must follow in order to achieve a goal at the end of the year. Children are also required to follow rules in school. They are expected to behave a certain way.

When I was growing up as a child I was disciplined sternly, with spankings and beatings from my father. I was rarely sat down and talked to in a calm, adult fashion about what is right and what is wrong. Unfortunately this was very common in some African-American households in the 1960s and 1970s. This was the way

DISCIPLINE

many African-Americans disciplined their children for many years. This method of discipline does not prepare our children to function as adults in society because we cannot always yell at or hit a person to get them to do what we want them to do. Sitting our children down and explaining to them what's right from what's wrong at an early age will prepare them for life as young adults and provide them a starting point for how to behave.

Once discipline is instilled in a child, it usually stays with them for the rest of their life. Rarely do you see a person who is disciplined change and become undisciplined. Once a person has experienced how much better their life is with discipline, they do not want to live without it.

Although my father was very strict, he was not always around to keep me from doing things I shouldn't be doing. As a result, I got into trouble at times when he was at work because I knew he wasn't watching me. On many occasions neighbors told my father the things I had done when he got home, and I paid later for doing those things. Joining the military was one of the best things that happened to me at an early age. When I first joined the military, they controlled every minute of every day of my life. I needed that.

I have raised two children. Both are adults, and both have college degrees. Achieving a college degree is a major accomplishment, because as a young adult you are expected to go away from home for the first time, study, and earn a degree in an environment where there are major distractions. Every year thousands of students drop out of college and the primary reason is a lack of focus and discipline. Discipline is doing the right thing when no one is watching, and no one is there to make you do what is right. I had to have a lot of discipline to walk away from those vendors who wanted me to steal money from the government when I was in the military. I refused to ruin my career and hurt my family.

SUCCEEDING WHILE BLACK

Many young adults, when left alone in a party environment, like most colleges and universities, simply do not have the discipline to study and stay focused like they're supposed to. We are all human and we all like to have fun, but we should never put aside things like schoolwork and other obligations to have a good time. Olympic runner Johnny Drummond went four years without eating candy to prepare for the 2000 Olympics. He could easily have snuck a piece of candy if he'd wanted to, but he had the discipline to stay away from it and train. Johnny's discipline helped him win a gold medal.

Commitment

Commitment is extremely important to success. Commitment is investing time and effort into whatever you are trying to do. When we commit to something, we agree to it and then obligate time and effort to it. It is very hard for young people to commit, because quite frankly, many of you are still trying to decide what you want to do. Even though I am very successful now and my life turned out fine, it surely was not due to my commitment; it was very hard for me to figure out what I wanted to do as a student in middle school and as a student in high school.

I recall going to my guidance counselor as a 10th grader, asking him what my options were in regard to college? I got a very rude awakening. After the guidance counselor pulled up my grades he told me my options for college, and the careers I was interested in were very limited. I was not overly surprised, but I realized that I had not applied myself in school, and it was going to cost me big time. This does not have to happen to you. You can start now by first being committed to your schoolwork, your grades, and your education--because as I stated earlier, a good education can separate you from the rest of the pack and it can propel you to great success.

Education is the foundation of success. The next thing you need to commit to is having a positive attitude. A smile and a good attitude will take you very far in life. I have seen what happens to people when they have poor attitudes. In most cases, the brightest and the smartest are sometimes overlooked, not hired for employment, or not selected for promotion because of having a poor attitude. Many times, people with mediocre or limited knowledge and abilities are given opportunities over more qualified individuals simply because they have a great attitude toward life, toward people, and toward their jobs.

People would much rather be around someone with a great attitude than around someone who is negative and rude. Committing to things is not easy, because a lot of times, some of the things we commit to we later find out are very hard, or time-consuming, and we want to give up. As children, we all remember how excited we were on the first day of school. I could barely sleep the night before, I had my school clothes out early, and I was just so anxious. This excitement for school usually lasts a few months. I also remember how I felt when April of the following year came around. I barely wanted to get out of bed. It was hard to stay focused--all of that excitement had gone away, but I remained in school and I stayed committed for those twelve years and earned a high school diploma.

The first twelve years of your education will be the hardest. You will go from a pre-kindergarten student who gets to play with toys and learn games, to an elementary school student who will start learning to read and write and get along with others, to a middle school student who is quickly becoming a young adult and will have to navigate through relationships. School not only prepares us for academics in life, but also teaches us how to live in a social setting, and how to deal with and avoid difficult people. When you finally become a high school student you are almost an adult that's ready to go out and survive in the real world. Those twelve years are really hard, and quite frankly, a lot of people don't make it through high school. African-Americans had a 57% high school graduation rate in 2009. One of the main purposes of this book is to keep you focused on your education so you can become successful. There is so much you can do with your life. There is so much you can conquer--but before you accomplish anything or take on any of

COMMITMENT

life's difficult tasks, you must first to commit to them.

When I think of commitment, the first person who comes to mind is Dr. Martin Luther King Jr. Here is a man who was so committed to his cause that he went to prison for that cause. He was threatened by people who wanted to harm him and his family for most of his life. He was eventually killed for his commitment to his cause. For an individual to be so committed to something, even when he knew it would eventually kill him, shows the ultimate commitment. I ask each and every one of you to commit to your education and to commit yourselves to having a positive attitude for the rest of your life.

Character

Like commitment, character is also important. Your character is all of the qualities, features, attributes, and behavior that shape who you are. People with good character excel in life. People with good character do what's right even when no one is watching them. People with good character make better friends, have better opportunities, are given more responsibility, and earn more money. Everyone loves and needs someone they can trust. Having good character and being an honest person is not easy; in fact, it is one of the hardest things to do and be.

There are so many outside influences that affect our character, but the biggest influence are our friends. We all want to fit in and be part of a group. Sometimes the desire to fit in causes us to do and say things we know we shouldn't...it also clouds our judgment. When I was twelve years old, my Little League baseball team won the city championship. As a reward, our team and the Colt League girls' team went on a trip to Carowinds, an amusement park in South Carolina. We were having a great time when one of the older girls asked me to steal some trinkets from one of the souvenir shops. I told her no at first, but some of my friends were stealing, the girls were pretty and I didn't want to seem like a scared little boy.

I followed her into the gift shop and she pointed out what she wanted me to steal: a key chain with a jug on the end. I picked up the key chain but didn't realize the chain part was hanging where it could be seen. As I walked out the door, one of the cashiers yelled, "Hey, you--come here!" I panicked and ran through the amusement

CHARACTER

park with two men chasing me. I tried to jump a small water channel and fell right in; the water went over my head.

I was pulled out of the water by the two men and taken into an interrogation room. I was soaked and scared to death. I was finally released to my coach, a muscular black man named Mr. Stewart. I could see the disappointment on my coach's face. Because I was a minor, I was released to my coach, but this was a big lesson for me. As I looked over at the girls who had asked me to steal for them, they were pointing and laughing at me as I stood there soaked, wet, and crying. I learned that stealing was wrong--but more importantly, I learned not to let people talk me into doing something I know to be wrong. You will face many situations in school and as an adult where your character will be tested. Sometimes it will be a friend or members of the opposite sex trying to persuade you to do something you know is wrong. There is nothing wrong with saying no. Sometimes you will have to leave some of your friends behind if you want to be successful.

Character flaws are a primary reason that so many young African-American males are in prison. African-American males make up a disproportionate number of people in prison. In 2009 there were 841 thousand black males in prison, more than there were in college. I tell the young African-American boys I mentor and talk to that once you are standing in front of a judge, you are in big trouble. You have put your destiny and your future in that judge's hand.

Integrity

Integrity is defined as "devotion to moral and ethical principles, honesty." Integrity and character go together. Integrity is important because having a good reputation is vital to being successful. Being honest and dependable can put you in a position for many opportunities not afforded to others. If you have integrity, people will trust you and work with you more easily. Truthfulness or dishonesty will determine how people interact with you at school, at home, and socially. If people cannot trust you, they will not include you. Integrity is also important when it comes to your schoolwork. There have been so many cases, recently, where individuals have been caught lying about their education. People have been portraying themselves as doctors, professors, and lawyers by using fake college transcripts.

There is also the plagiarizing of documents off the internet. Many students in grade school and college are using the internet to steal papers and speeches to use as their own. There is a certain amount of satisfaction that comes from doing your own schoolwork or any work for that matter. You get feeling of pride and accomplishment when you put in the work yourself. Being honest is especially important when you are dealing with your parents.

I will never forget the time I stole my father's car. It was right before he was going to trade it in. It was a 1968 Pontiac Bonneville. While my father was at work I grabbed the keys and took the car for a drive around the block. The drive was fine until I tried to park the car in the driveway. While backing the car in, I hit our back stairs, which were made out of metal. This put a huge dent on the

INTEGRITY

driver's side of the car. As you can imagine, I was terrified of my father finding out. Two people came and test drove the car after I parked it, which gave me a way to get out of the situation I was in. When my father got home, he thought one of the people who test drove the car put the dent in it. I was too scared to tell the truth, so I let him believe that. It hurt me to lie to him and let someone else take the blame for what I had done. I finally told my dad the truth years later, but it was too late; I should have told the truth back when it happened. You will have many situations in life where you will be faced with telling the truth or telling a lie. Even though it may be hard to do, telling the truth is always the best choice. When you tell one lie, you usually have to tell more lies to cover up the first one.

During my military career I was trusted with hundreds of thousands of dollars. There were many occasions when I had opportunities to put some of that money in my pocket. Sometimes when I would pay vendors they would ask me if I wanted to forge receipts for services? I always turned them down flat. Had I done this, I would have surely been caught, which would have put my military career in jeopardy and hurt my family. When you are faced with the opportunity to steal, lie, or cheat--walk away.

Work Ethic

Work ethic is defined as "a set of values based on hard work." These values are not just related to a job, but to everything we do in life. Work ethic can be applied to how we approach schoolwork, athletics, and many other events where preparation is required. Hard work is what America was built on. As we enter the technology age there have been a lot of physical labor type jobs done away with in our society. Regardless of what type of work you do, be it physical labor or technology-based, preparation is still required--hard work is still required. It is never too early to learn the value of hard work. As students, you can start now by studying, practicing, and preparing for a test and the day-to-day lessons you'll learn in school. All of the success that I have comes from hard work. Being a black man in the special operations community and the military, you constantly have to prove yourself. There have been many occasions throughout my military and civilian careers where I had to work harder than my counterparts of other ethnicities because of what I looked like. There were other times when I was passed over for promotions and leadership positions for people who were less qualified than I was at the time. These disappointments did not make me bitter, only more disciplined and focused. I have learned never to reveal when I am upset about something to people. It is important always to be in control of your emotions.

Many African-Americans today seem to focus on entertainers and sports stars as role models, and as examples of careers they wish to pursue. While both of these career fields pay well, becoming a professional athlete or entertainer is very difficult to achieve. Even entertainers and athletes have to work hard to be successful. Entertainers have to rehearse constantly, travel, and be without

WORK ETHIC

their families for long periods of time. Athletes have to eat right, work out constantly, study game film, travel, and be without their families as well. A strong work ethic is required to be successful at any goal or career you pursue.

A strong work ethic is what built this country. Many of our ancestors worked long hard hours for little pay so that young people today can have an education and part of the American dream. Our ancestors would be disappointed if they could see some of the behavior some of our African-American youth are displaying. We are blaming everyone but ourselves for our problems, and many of us refuse to work because we feel certain jobs are beneath us or are disgraceful. No honest wage-paying job is disgraceful. If I had to go to work in the fast food industry right now, I would do that in a heartbeat if that was the only way I could feed my family. We were poor growing up, but my father was too proud to accept public assistance; he worked two jobs. I remember going with my father to his job as a janitor and how hard he worked, and how proud he was. My father didn't have a glamorous job or make a lot of money, but he took a lot of pride in what he did. I am glad my father took me to work with him. We must regain our pride in the work we do, regardless of what type work that is.

The five principles I just talked about are vital to your success as an African-American. Start applying them today and you will see a big improvement in all aspects of your life: school, work, productivity, success, and overall happiness. African-Americans need to stop being lazy and take pride in their work, be it at school or on the job. We can no longer make excuses and blame everyone else for our failures and lack of success. African-Americans in this country have rights and opportunities to get an education and achieve success like everyone else if they are willing to work hard. There are other minorities who have come to America, worked hard, and flourished. It is time we African-Americans do the same.

Appearance

Mentoring Banquet 2012

There is a saying that we are being judged by the way we look long before we ever speak a single word. I truly believe that. In fact, there are many occasions where people are never given opportunities to speak because of the way they look. Although it may not be fair, it's just the way life is. People judge you based on what you look like.

Most young African-Americans are being negatively stereotyped because of their style. Sagging pants, gold teeth, tattoos and dreadlocks are some of the styles that are the cause of this negative stereotyping. I personally don't judge people by the way they dress, and I don't have a problem with any of the aforementioned clothing if worn at the right time and place.

I remember being a teenager and wearing an afro in the seventies. An afro was the hairstyle worn by of a lot of militants during those days--Angela Davis, Black Panthers, etc.... However, many people do judge young African-Americans by the way they dress. Many of

APPEARANCE

our youth are denied a good education, service at businesses, and opportunities for employment because they are presumed to be thugs based on what they look like.

Young African-Americans need to learn what to wear and when and how to wear it! When you are hanging out with your friends or family, casual dress is fine. However, when you go out in public to school, church, or to a restaurant, you should wear decent clothes, and not bring negative attention to yourself by wearing clothes that are not appropriate.

You should never be feared you because of the way you are dressed. You should always dress properly when you are applying for a job or any other interview. Like I said earlier, most people make up their minds about you as soon as they see you.

Wearing decent clothes does not make you a sellout. I have heard this many times, and I don't understand why young people feel this way. If you want to succeed in life, you have to put some effort into your appearance. This includes grooming your hair, and personal hygiene. A well-dressed, well-groomed person is more respected by everyone who comes in contact with them, and it opens up opportunities.

Lastly, you do not have to be ashamed if you can't afford the latest pair of expensive tennis shoes or latest fashion gear. The parents of many of the kids you are in school with can't afford that stuff either. They are putting themselves in debt to buy these clothes for their children just so they can fit in or boast about being in fashion.

Be happy with what you have. I did not grow up with the best clothes; in fact, I used to get teased a lot in school for the clothes I wore. Now when I visit my home town, most of the people who teased me can't afford to dress better than me now. Be thankful for and take care of the clothes you have. Your parents are doing the best they can; you don't need to put pressure on them to buy you the latest and most expensive clothes. Whatever you wear, please wear it in a decent respectful manner. People are judging you based on what you look like as well as how you conduct yourself. Your appearance matters.

Finances

My Current Home

Managing and understanding your money is essential to your success. Most African-Americans rarely discuss finances with their children. When I say discuss, I mean teach our children the value of a dollar and how to save for their future. Many of us struggle financially and it is hard to teach your children about something you don't have. However, many African-Americans were never taught the value of a dollar and how to save by their parents, either.

Some African-Americans tend to put a priority on owning material things rather than investing, saving for the future, and home ownership. I currently live in a nice community, and few of my neighbors are African-American. African-American homeowners make up just 20% of homeowners in the United States. When you look at the contributions that African-Americans have made to this country, we as a people should be in a much better status, financially. When I'm traveling around this great country of ours, I usually pay attention to what people are reading. I rarely see an African-American reading any type of financial publication. African-Americans need to read and learn more about finances, and live by the basic fundamental that you don't spend more money than you make. If all Americans did this one simple thing, we wouldn't have all the financial problems we have in this country today. The recession in 2008 was brought on by greed, and people living above their means.

Most young African-Americans today tend to focus a lot on style and fashion, and there is nothing wrong with that. When I was a young boy we cared a lot about fashion too, but we did not spend more money on clothing and other things than we could afford.

Black youth tend to focus on style and fashion at any cost--how do you explain people getting run over at a store for a pair of $180 tennis shoes? I do not blame the children for this activity. This responsibility lies solely on the parents. When I was a young boy, my father would tell me "no" without concern if I asked for things we could not afford. I will never forget the time my father refused to buy me a pair of $10 tennis shoes. I had to work to come up with half the money to buy those shoes. They were a pair of Converse Chuck Taylors. I took great care of them because they were so hard to come by. Nowadays, children get a new pair of sneakers sometimes twice a year.

Today it seems that parents want to be accepted by their children rather than discipline and teach them the hard facts of life. Some parents today will buy their children anything--even things they know they can't afford--to make their children happy. There is nothing wrong with parents telling their children "no" sometimes. "No" is a word they should hear often. They will surely hear the word "no" often when they go out into the world on their own.

African-Americans should save or invest a percentage of everything you earn, even if it's a small amount of your pay. You will be

FINANCES

surprised how fast money grows when you start saving. Learning to save money at an early age will teach you how much power having your own money brings. I have been earning my own money since I was a young boy around eleven years old. I mowed lawns, sold bottles, and carried people's groceries to their car for them. I always had my own money to buy the things I wanted. I rarely had to ask my father for money for candy and other treats. When I was old enough to legally work, I got a job at a supermarket. I bought all my own school clothes and paid for my own entertainment. My working really helped my father out a lot. There is nothing wrong with having nice clothes and the latest technology, as long as you don't put your family in financial despair paying for them. Having your own money gives you financial independence.

Social Media

Social media is a part of everyday life now. You cannot go anywhere without seeing someone with a smart phone or tablet checking Facebook, Twitter, or their LinkedIn accounts. Social media is here to stay, and can be a valuable tool for business, or staying in touch with old friends.

Many African-Americans are jeopardizing, and risking, future opportunities based on the content they are placing on social media. When I was growing up we were taught to be private, and keep our business to ourselves. Today, people are sharing everything on sites like Twitter and Facebook. People put racy photos, filthy language, unpleasant things about their employers, and other content that can embarrass themselves and be used against them later on their jobs, and later in life.

I have Facebook, Twitter, and a LinkedIn account. I have these accounts because I need them as a business owner, and they are a great way to stay connected with family and old friends from my days in the military. However I'm very careful about the information, pictures, and other content I share on these sites. Once you put something on one of these sites it will be around forever, and many of these things can come back to haunt you later in life, if you're looking for a job, applying to a college, or running for political office.

Can you imagine what this world would be like if Facebook and Twitter had been around 50 to 100 years ago? I guarantee you,

SOCIAL MEDIA

history would have been written differently, because a lot of things that happened during those years never came to light because there was no mass media to let everyone know. Now we live in a time where we know things as soon as they happen and that can be good and bad. Social media is a way of life now, and it can be a lot of fun, but we have to remember that not everything we do needs to be shared with the rest of the world. Use caution and self-control when posting content to social media websites.

Mentoring

Mentoring Banquet with boys With Mayor Chavonne and Mentees 2012

I have been a mentor of young African-American boys for several years now. I can tell you that our young men are in a lot of trouble. Many young African-American men today do not care about education, their appearance, or hard work, and many of them do not have respect for their elders or women. This does not apply to all young black men--I know there are some young African-American males out there trying to do the right thing who are the complete opposite of the young men I spoke of earlier.

Many young African-American boys in this country are being raised by women. These women are doing the best they can, but they face tough challenges, especially when a boy becomes a teenager. Some women baby their sons to the point where they can't function in society. These young men feel they are entitled, and feel like everything should be done for them. If you are doing everything and making excuses for your son, stop it now. You are not helping him by doing this. People in the real word expect him to act like a man,

MENTORING

and they will treat him like a man, not like you have been treating him at home.

I have been a mentor at a local Youth Academy for five years. I have seen angry young men come into our program and turn their lives around in a few years with the help and guidance of positive African-American male role models. Any time that you can spend with a young child is worth more than you can imagine. The problem is that there just aren't enough mentors. When I was a boy, every man in my neighborhood was basically a mentor. They made sure we stayed out of trouble. They made sure we were behaving ourselves, and they made sure we were always safe and taken care of. All a child needs to flourish is for someone to take care of them and look out for them. I encourage everyone to become a mentor to a child or support mentoring organizations. Do it today. There is a child out there that needs you.

Leadership

At the Dr. King Memorial 2012

I believe leadership, and the lack thereof, is at the forefront of all of the world's problems. I said the world, not the United States of America, not Africa. Not Australia--I said the world.

We live in a time now where everyone likes to follow. No one wants to lead--leadership takes courage, leadership takes strength, leadership takes a person who is willing to risk his own life if need be to do what's right for a cause. Where have men like Dr. King gone? What I see today is a lot of African-American leaders making excuses. The year is 2012, we have a black president, and you would think this would uplift the African-American people, motivate them to become successful, motivate them to work hard, and motivate young African-American males to lead, not follow. When I sit in meetings at my job, sometimes I'm the only African-American in the room. There is no one else who looks like me in the room. That should not be!

President Obama is one man trying to do the best he can. But as we all know, the president can do only so much. He has to work with the Congress, and he has to work with other nations. I have never seen the type of hatred and verbal venom expressed toward

LEADERSHIP

any president during my lifetime as I see in the way people talk about President Obama. I was in the military during Jimmy Carter's presidency. Things were so bad during that time we had to turn the lights out during the day to save power. All of the vehicles in our motor pool were broken. Throughout all of that, I never heard one person in uniform complain about Jimmy Carter. Now we have a state-of-the-art military. We have a pretty good country by most standards, and all I hear is negativity expressed directly toward the president. While I don't want to believe it, I know a lot of this venom is directed at him because he is an African-American. Many Americans thought we would never have a black president, and many don't want one.

African-Americans should be prepared for conflict, rejection, dismissal, and inequality. Now when I say prepare yourself for these, I'm saying that during your lifetime you will experience all of the things I mentioned above. But if you're prepared for it, if you understand it, and if you understand the people who are doing these things to you, you'll be able to deal with and handle it. You will be able to persevere, and you will be able to become successful. Take President Obama as an example: during his run for the presidency in 2008, the Democrats and the Republicans threw everything including the kitchen sink at him. President Obama was prepared, and he fought off every attack, one by one: Reverend Wright, being a Muslim, being born in Kenya, being a socialist, and being inexperienced.

Most African-American men I know could not have put up with these kinds of attacks without retaliation. But Barack Obama repealed these attacks. He eloquently fought off these attacks, and the American people saw something that they had never seen before in a black man. They saw a black man that could control his emotions, a black man who spoke with a calm confidence, a black man who had the audacity and the courage to lead. The world needs a lot more men like Barack Obama in all walks of life, not just in the Oval Office. To all my young African-American brothers out there, this is your call: it is time to wake up. You can enjoy your music, you can enjoy social media, you can enjoy everything that modern pop culture offers, but you have to get an education. You have to respect women and your elders. You have to work hard and you have to turn the tide on this new culture of incarceration and plain ignorance. It is time for young black men to step up and make people like Dr. King--who came before you and sacrificed so much-- proud. I have been fortunate enough to meet a president and a vice president. And I will tell you that they are men just like you and me--the only difference is that these men are driven. They are focused, and they work very hard; they have set a goal and they go out to achieve that goal. It is time for African-American males to pull together to help one another, to mentor one another, to lead one another to that promised land that Dr. King talked about so many years ago. We need you now. It is time to lead.

Teen Pregnancy

Don't do it! Teen pregnancy has been a problem in our society, and especially in the black community, for many years. Teen pregnancy doesn't affect just African-Americans; it affects the entire country. Teen pregnancy comes from a lack of understanding and education of the consequences of having a baby, when you're still a baby yourself. I've raised two daughters, and I often talked with them and pleaded with them to not jeopardize their futures by becoming pregnant while they were teenagers. I do realize accidents do happen, especially when two very young people get caught up in the moment, but teenagers should refrain from having sex if at all possible.

I know there are young women out there who have become successful, earned college degrees, and earned a good living after becoming pregnant early in life, but those young women are the exceptions, not the rule. While there are some teen mothers who get their educations and become successful, there are many others who struggle. They struggle to raise their children, they struggle to finish their educations, and they struggle to earn a living and survive. Many of them face their struggles alone, with the boy who impregnated them nowhere to be found.

For the young men out there: it is time to stop reproducing just because you think it's cool or just because you are too lazy to use protection. The children you are bringing into this world are growing up without a father, without a future, and sometimes without hope. Many of these children will wind up uneducated, unprepared, and without much hope for a successful future.

Abstaining from sex, using protection, and being there for your children is part of that leadership I was talking about earlier. For all you young African-American ladies, before you decide to have a child, please do some research--talk to other mothers who had children when they were very young. Ask them about their struggles and challenges. Raising children is a joy, but it is very hard work. I remember working two jobs to support my family, because I didn't want my wife to work while my kids couldn't talk. I was a soldier during the day; I drove a pizza truck at night. I did not want to do that, but it was necessary to support my family. Leadership is about doing what you have to do because you know its right.

For those who are with child, or if you're becoming a young father for the first time, I want you to know your life is not over. You can still become successful, but you have to give up a lot to achieve that success. You have to give up some of the freedoms you would have as a normal teenager. This is a problem I see with many young parents today. They want to leave their children with someone else--usually their parents--while they continue to party and do the things teenagers without children do.

I was a teenager once, and I know what it's like when you're hormones start to rage. But remember, a child is a commitment for eighteen years or maybe longer. That is a very long commitment for a few minutes of pleasure. Please think about that the next time you think about having sex or getting pregnant. Please abstain from having sex until you're a responsible adult. Please think about your future before you decide to have unprotected sex. Remember, a child is an 18+ year commitment.

Success and the African-American

Speaking in 2009

I am definitely not the most successful African-American on the planet. I don't compare to President Obama. I don't compare to Oprah Winfrey. I don't compare to many of the entertainers and African-American athletes out there.

I have, however, attained a great amount of success considering the odds I had to face. I achieved my success by working hard, getting an education, reading, being prepared--and most importantly, treating people the right way, with dignity and respect. I have traveled, all over the world, fathered two wonderful children who are successful, both of whom have their college degrees. I have had successful careers in the military, in the corporate world, in broadcasting, and in business. I have a beautiful home, nice cars and a great lifestyle. I've been able to achieve all of this by simply being prepared, working hard and treating people right.

SUCCEEDING WHILE BLACK

Many young people today don't view people with a normal jobs and normal responsibilities as being a success. When I say normal jobs I am talking about jobs that are not glamorous. I don't understand why some young people look down on everyday workers who support their families with normal jobs, but it's something we need to stop doing. Not everyone can be a pro athlete, an entertainer, or someone famous who makes millions of dollars. My father had a saying: you can't miss something you never had. The person who works an everyday job and does that job with pride and works hard is often just as happy as those millionaire athletes--sometimes even happier.

You should not feel like a failure just because you don't have a big house and a fancy car. This mindset is what caused the financial crisis in 2008. That financial crisis was caused by greed on both sides--both Wall Street and the American public--who were purchasing homes and acquiring lifestyles through credit that they knew they could not afford. These people bought large houses with adjustable mortgages under faulty lending practices by the major banks in this country. When the banks failed, the American people had to bail them out. This should have been a lesson to all, but some of those trends continue today. We as African-Americans have to do better. We have to start saving instead of spending. We have to stop being so materialistic and spending our money on things of no value. We have to leave something for our children.

If you work hard at whatever you do, you'll be successful. Many of the athletes and entertainers we idolize, from Oprah to Kobe Bryant to Beyoncé, all work extremely hard to achieve and maintain their success. Much of this hard work is put in behind the scenes, and all we see is them shining on television. They did not achieve their level of success by sitting on their butts and being lazy. You have to put in effort and work hard to be successful. Webster's dictionary defines success as "a favorable or desired outcome."

SUCCESS AND THE AFRICAN-AMERICAN

Success and good results do not always mean wealth and fame. We must stop equating success to having a lot of money and having a lot of material possessions.

You will rarely find a successful person who does not read. I believe a person who doesn't read is no better off than a person who can't. Successful people read daily to stay abreast of current events and to be on top of their game. You should try to read something every day of your life, be it the newspaper, a book, or a blog on the internet. Reading stimulates the mind, forces us to think, and causes reactions. Reading can motivate us to succeed.

Most people who are successful have a positive attitude toward everything in life. I cannot stress enough how important your attitude is. Your attitude will determine your outcome; it dictates how you perform, and dictates how your life will go. No one wants to be around someone with a poor attitude--attitude is everything. Being successful and black is not easy. There are always distractions: people wanting to take your job, discredit you, and disobey your orders. African-Americans need to understand that things will always be different for us. Even after you achieve success, there are some people who will never respect you. This is a part of life as an African-American, and something you have to learn to deal with.

Conduct in the Workplace

I have had over twenty jobs in my lifetime. I have seen a lot of disturbing behavior amongst my coworkers, both black and white. What I want to talk about now is the behavior of African-Americans in the workplace. When you are hired to do a job, you are expected to perform that job to the best of your ability. I have seen people show up to work and act like they are doing the boss a favor by being there. I've also seen people show up to work with horrible attitudes, improperly dressed, and very late. All of these behaviors contribute to the negative stereotypes that African-Americans have, especially in the workplace.

Another problem amongst some African-Americans in the workplace is anger, and combativeness. I have also seen bullying and disrespecting behavior toward supervisors and coworkers. We spend almost as much time at work as we do at home. Our jobs should be a safe, fun, and positive environment. There will be times when your coworkers and supervisors will make your work environment almost unbearable, but that is not an excuse to lose control of your emotions and become part of the problem.

In order to be successful in the workplace, you must be on time. This may be the most important thing you can do as an employee. Being on time shows you are serious about your job, and it shows you want to be there. Being late for work can ruin your entire day, not to mention the business you work for and their customers. Work schedules are made for a reason. Your boss needs you there on time to be ready to go when your shift starts. I always show up ten minutes prior to my reporting time for everything. If you have

CONDUCT IN THE WORKPLACE

to be at work at 8:00, show up at 7:50.

Your attitude in the workplace is also very important. You should always try to show up to work with a good attitude. We all have bad days, but it does not hurt to smile and be pleasant to your coworkers and customers. This is especially true if you have a job working with the public and dealing with customers. No one wants to deal with an employee with a horrible attitude. We have to remember that even when we are having a bad day, we owe it to customers and our coworkers to be polite and have a good attitude.

There are so many people out there, young and old, who do not know how to conduct themselves in the workplace. There are some discussions we should never have at work: our private lives, love lives, our problems, and other personal business should never be discussed. However, I witness people talking about these things all the time while I'm out shopping or dining at restaurants. Unfortunately African-Americans are usually the loudest. No one cares about your business; tone it down and keep it to yourself.

The other thing we must understand about the workplace is that it is very competitive. Everyone you work with is trying to advance or look good in the eyes of their supervisors. Your coworkers are trying to better themselves, and you are sometimes viewed as the competition. Talking too much and discussing your personal issues can sometimes make it straight to your boss via one of your coworkers. Employees with personal issues are rarely chosen to lead other people.

Everything you do or say in the workplace is being watched or listened to. All of your actions can be used to evaluate your performance and to decide if you remain employed, are given a raise, or are promoted to a higher position. This process starts on your first day on the job and continues throughout your life!

I truly believe that the less you talk in life the better off you will be. I have not always lived by this, but I have learned over the years that silence is truly golden. Most African-Americans talk way too much in the workplace. Most of this talk is about nonsense and activities that are not suited for discussions on the job. Loss of promotions and raises are usually the outcome from talking too much on the job.

Employers hire you to do a job, not to come to their business to socialize and talk about what you do in your off time. I have worked many jobs in my life, and I have been successful because I don't share too much personal information and I try not to talk too much. I have always understood that first and foremost I was there to do a job. I am not saying you shouldn't talk at all in the workplace. I am only saying you should be careful what you say, whom you say it to, and when you say it.

Please take your job seriously, no matter what it is. I always find it interesting that some look down on people who work in the fast food industry, yet we all dine at these fast food restaurants, and many of us entered the workforce for the first time at these restaurants. Never be embarrassed about making an honest living.

When you report for work, go there with a positive attitude, and be as productive as you can be. Believe me--if you do this, it will pay off. I have been able to achieve success because I have always taken my job seriously, worked hard, and overprepared. You can be successful too, if you apply the same approach to everything you do.

The Obama Factor

On Tuesday January 20, 2009 it snowed so much that the city of Fayetteville, North Carolina and all surrounding areas were shut down. Most businesses and all schools were also closed. It was inauguration day and in a few hours the United States would have its first black president.

This was something I thought I would never see in my lifetime. Every black candidate who had run for this office prior to Barack Obama had fallen far short, most not even making it halfway through the primaries. There was Shirley Chisholm; a New York teacher elected to the US House of Representatives...Chisholm unsuccessfully sought the Democratic presidential nomination in 1972. She did get the most convention votes (152) for a female candidate in US history.

Jesse Jackson had campaigned for the Democratic nomination twice, in 1984 and 1988. Jackson won several primaries and had respectable runs during both campaigns. These runs made Jackson one of the top black American leaders during the eighties.

There was Lenora Fulani. In 1988, Fulani—a psychologist—ran as an independent and was the first black woman to appear on presidential ballots in all fifty states. She also ran in 1992.

Alan Keyes--after serving in the Reagan administration, Keyes campaigned for the Republican nomination in 1996 and 2000 (he also lost to Barack Obama in their race for a Senate seat in 2004).

SUCCEEDING WHILE BLACK

US senator Carol Moseley Braun briefly sought the Democratic presidential nomination in 2004.

And there was Al Sharpton. In 2004, this New York-based activist campaigned for the Democratic presidential nomination.

Where all of these African-Americans failed, a young well-educated senator from Chicago did not. Barack Obama shocked the world by winning the Iowa caucuses on January 3, 2008 and continued winning primaries all the way to the White House.

Along the way Obama was called everything from a terrorist and a racist to a socialist and an illegal alien. Until 2011, when the president finally produced his birth certificate, there were still millions of Americans who thought Obama had been born in Kenya. One of my Tea Party coworkers put an Obama Kenyan birth certificate on my desk; of course it was an internet fake!

Obama handled all of the insults and criticism with dignity and grace. He never got upset and he never lost his cool. We can all learn a lot from the way the president dealt with adversity during his campaign and while in office. I don't always agree with all of his policies, but I truly admire the way he conducts himself. President Obama should be an inspiration for all African-Americans.

How fitting it was that on this inauguration day, January 20, 2009 the snow was so deep that every child and adult in our city got a chance to see an event that many thought would never happen: the swearing-in of the first black President of the United States. I will forever remember how proud I was that day; I doubt that any black man alive didn't feel some sense of pride. I cried that day; Inauguration Day 2009 was simply awesome.

I was sure that with the election of an African-American president, our people would view life and the world through a different lens. I was also sure that Barack Obama's ascension to the presidency would bring Americans together. Our newfound hope and pride would surely motivate African-Americans to reach new heights academically, socially, and economically.

I thought this event would surely change the future of all our generations. To this day, I still don't think most African-Americans understand the symbolism of what having Obama in the White House means; it means African-Americans can do anything. Most of us have no desire to be POTUS, but after seeing Obama overcome all the odds he faced, there should be nothing too hard for any African-American to achieve, if they put their minds to it and work hard.

Unfortunately, African-Americans have not excelled as much as I had hoped; I was sure that Obama's election would inspire many young Americans to take education more seriously and become more active in the American political process. But many of the young people I talk to and mentors are not interested at all in politics, and are not doing much better in school, either. Twenty percent of blacks twenty-five and older had a bachelor's degree or higher in 2008, compared to eighteen percent in 2010. The annual median income of black households in 2007 was $33,916 compared to $32,068 in 2010. There are more statistics that show blacks' lack of progress since President Obama was elected.

Another myth that arose was that racism would go away because America had elected a black president. I think we have all seen that this is simply not true. There are examples of racism displayed almost every day; some are subtle and some are blatant. Despite all the statistics and false beliefs, African-Americans should still use President Obama's election as fuel to propel them to succeed. We have come a long way, but we still have a long way to go. There are still people who don't believe that the president is a US citizen. I don't ever recall anyone questioning the citizenship of any of our other presidents.

Throughout all of the negativity and his historic battles with Congress, President Obama has conducted himself with dignity and grace. Most people would have responded in some way to all of the negativity that has been directed toward the president, but Barack Obama just brushed it all of his shoulder. I truly believe his character and his grace are what got him re-elected in 2012. Young African-American men can learn a lot from the president.

No More Excuses

Youth Speech 2010

There are many reasons why my life could have turned out differently. When my mother died I almost gave up hope; my father was uneducated and abused alcohol; and we were poor. I felt sorry for myself a lot, and I didn't want to get out of bed on most days.

There were many kids in my neighborhood living in similar circumstances; we dealt with our situations, and had fun for the most part. I learned early in life that you cannot make excuses for your life situation. I believe we will all be tested and challenged at some point in our lives. Some of us are born into better situations than others, but we all have an opportunity to be successful in life. With an education and hard work, anything is possible. Look at our president; he came from very humble beginnings. He also came from a single-parent home. While not everyone can become President of the United States, we can all get an education and become productive members of society. There is always someone in a worse situation than the one we are in. Making excuses doesn't help us reach our goals. Don Wilder once said, "Excuses are the nails used to build a house of failure."

The fact that we now have a black president is not the only reason African-Americans need to quit making excuses for our lack of equality. There are many other minorities who have come to America and succeeded. Asians, Indians, and other ethnicities have come to this country, worked hard, and opened successful businesses through hard work and discipline, and are thriving in this country.

African-Americans can no longer afford do play the victim. We need to focus on education and discipline when it comes to raising our children and managing our finances. We also need to start opening businesses in our neighborhoods, start supporting each other, and stop stealing from and doing harm to each other. Most of the crime committed in the African-American community is done by the people who live in those communities. I drove by a house the other day that had bars on all the windows. People should not have to bar themselves in their own homes to keep their personal possessions safe.

There is no doubt that African-Americans have experienced hardships in America. However, we can no longer blame others for our lack of progress or success. We now have the same opportunities everyone else has. We are not entitled to anything. Dr. King, Medgar Evers, Rosa Parks, and many others made sacrifices for civil rights and equality for African-Americans in this country. We are repaying them by acting like a race of people who have forgotten about those sacrifices, and many of us are behaving in ways that dishonor our great civil rights leaders and African-American heroes. Now is the time to turn things around. Now is the time to *Succeed While Black*.

Summary

New York City 2007

I have talked about many cures for the problems I feel many African-Americans face today. I have talked about my upbringing, the challenges I faced growing up, the many mistakes I made and how I almost threw my life away by not taking school seriously.

I have also talked about some surefire cures to fix much of what's wrong with our people.

We have to start putting a value on education, hard work and respecting our families. It's time to start putting in the hard work to achieve the success you want in life.

There is a black family living in the White House. I don't think most African-Americans really understand what that means. What is means is there are no longer any excuses for not achieving your dreams. President Obama fought through one of the most bitter, and negative campaigns in our countries history to win the presidential election in 2008. He had to fight even harder to get re-elected in 2012. Throughout all of the negative campaigning and personal attacks the President conducted himself with class and grace.

Barack Obama's ascension to the presidency should motivate every African-American in this country to work hard, and achieve their goals. No more excuses.

I have been very critical of African-Americans, our behavior, the way we are performing and conducting ourselves in this book. My criticism is not part of any agenda; neither does it come from self loathing. I am extremely proud to be an African-American. The sole purpose of my criticism is to motivate African-Americans to return to a time when education, community and hard work were more important than bling, cell phones and tennis shoes.

> "A goal without a plan is a wish"
> Unknown

www.ingramcontent.com/pod-product-compliance
Lightning Source LLC
Chambersburg PA
CBHW070313110426
42738CB00052B/2534